SUPER SKILLS

HOW TO BE A BLOGGER AND VLOGGER IN 10 EASY LESSONS

SHANE BIRLEY

Walter Foster Jr.

Quarto is the authority on a wide range of topics. Quarto educates, entertains and enriches the lives of our readers— enthusiasts and lovers of hands-on living. www.quartoknows.com

© Marshall Editions Children's Books 2016
Part of The Quarto Group
The Old Brewery
6 Blundell Street
London N7 9BH

First published in the UK in 2016 by QED Publishing

Published in the USA by Walter Foster Jr.,
an imprint of Quarto Publishing Group USA Inc.
All rights reserved. Walter Foster Jr. is trademarked.

Publisher: Maxime Boucknooghe
Art Director: Susi Martin
Editorial Director: Laura Knowles
Design: Clare Barber
Original Illustrations: Joanna Kerr

6 Orchard Road, Suite 100
Lake Forest, CA 92630
quartoknows.com
Visit our blogs @quartoknows.com

ABOUT THE AUTHOR

Shane Birley is a seasoned blogger with a technical background and a degree in Literature. He has combined these talents to co-author several editions of Blogging for Dummies. He also founded Left Right Minds, a web development and technology consulting company based in Vancouver, Canada.

Printed in China
1 3 5 7 9 10 8 6 4 2

CONTENTS

WELCOME TO THE WORLD OF BLOGGING

Blogging is everywhere. Newspapers, television programs, celebrities, and everyday individuals use blogging to promote, share, and express their ideas all the time. Using audio, video, and text, blogs have become one of the most popular ways to share information online. Why not join in? Sharing your story has never been easier—all you need to do is let your creativity out! In this book, you will experiment and discover the blogging method that suits you the best.

Are you ready?

Of course you are! You already have experiences worth telling other people about. Maybe you read a great book that excited you, or learned a new skill in class. Perhaps you discovered something unknown in your own hometown, or even visited another country. You may be surprised, but people love reading and hearing about other people's adventures. It's what makes blogging a great resource for sharing stories and learning new things. You can be inspired by other bloggers or inspire and enlighten them.

HANDY TIP!

Starting your own blog can feel like a big project, so take it one step at a time.

IT'S EASY WHEN YOU BREAK IT DOWN

This book will introduce you to the 10 core skills for blogging. You'll get the most out of it if you read the chapters in order and try out the practical activities that are suggested. As you become more confident in your blogging, look back through the skills to practice the discussed techniques and try out new things.

WORDS, VIDEO, AUDIO...
THE CHOICE IS YOURS!

In this book, we are going to talk about writing posts, recording audio, taking photographs, and shooting video to enhance your storytelling. Mixing these elements will make your stories interesting and exciting, giving your followers a reason to visit your blog again and again. Together, we will review all the types of technology that you can use to help tell your story.

- -

YOUR VOICE IS UNIQUE

Being confident in your blog and embracing your own view of the world will make creating your blog that much easier. If you are excited about what you share with your blog visitors, they will be excited too. No matter what type of blog you decide to create, it all begins with sorting out your ideas. Plan what you want to say and how you want to say it. Working through this book will help you find your own voice.

IMPORTANT: YOU MUST BE 13 YEARS OLD OR OLDER TO JOIN MOST BLOGGING AND SOCIAL MEDIA SITES. ALWAYS ASK PERMISSION FROM YOUR PARENTS.

ONE OF THE MOST IMPORTANT PARTS OF BLOGGING IS TO HAVE FUN. SMILE, THINK OF POSITIVE THINGS, AND **GET PLANNING!**

FIND YOUR STORY

Bloggers love to tell stories, but telling a story can be one of the hardest things to do. Where do you start? How should you tell it? What will make your story interesting? Many bloggers often worry that the story they want to tell is too boring and wonder why anyone would want to hear about their life. The reality is that readers love to read about other people's experiences. They like to take part in other people's adventures and interests, and they want to learn—from you too! Your experiences are unique!

GETTING STARTED

Let's do some brainstorming. Grab a piece of paper and a pencil to jot a few things down in a list. Write down 10 things that you like to do or love to talk about. Don't be shy! Some people like to talk about films while others like to describe their favorite places to go horseback riding. The things on this list could be anything. Let your mind wander and don't hold back! If you get stuck, you can always ask a friend or family member to help you.

WHATEVER COMES OUT, JUST **WRITE IT DOWN!**

* * MY IDEAS * *

Movies I LOVE ♡

Balloon animals I can make

My bucket list

My cat is the smartest cat in the universe!

Can I have a vacation on the moon?

Magnetic poetry: GOOD or BAD?

My favorite science fiction books

Paper airplanes and the future of flight.

Watch me brush my teeth

My top photographs I have taken

MAKE A MIND MAP

Thinking about your interests for the first time can be difficult. After all, talking to complete strangers about yourself and the things you like can be mind-boggling. Another trick you can use is a mind map, where you draw your ideas in a collection of circles. Drawing circles can help you visualize connections you may not see from a list of your interests.

First write down a blog topic and draw a circle around it. Then write another topic outside of the circle you just made and draw a circle around that word. Are the topics similar? Are they the same subject? If they are related, draw a line between the two circles to connect them. Keep writing new topics and connecting them to related circles. The topic with the greatest number of connections will probably be the one that you know a lot about.

PRACTICE, PRACTICE, PRACTICE!

A lot of people say that practice makes perfect—they are right! If you want to become good at anything, you need to practice and experiment to become an expert. Putting your pen to paper is always a good start, but coming up with ideas to practice may require a little inspiration. Open up a newspaper or look at some news articles online (the happier the better!). Write down your thoughts about what you read.

Call up a friend to ask for their opinion and write down their ideas. If the news isn't your thing, try writing about a book you are reading or the music you are listening to. How do books or music make you feel? Or you can try imagining what it would be like if you met a famous person. What would you say to them? Write out an imaginary conversation you would want to have. Keeping your mind actively thinking is the key. When you fill it up with information, your thoughts can spill out through your pen.

HANDY TIP!

Putting a limit on your ideas can be a good way of focusing on what you really want to write about. Time yourself for a minute and brainstorm within that time. At the end of the minute, you can review the list and decide on a blog post or a topic for your blog!

TIME TO EXPERIMENT

When you sit down to plan out your blog for the first time, it may seem like an impossible task. But all you really need to do is play with your ideas, write, and record without any plan at all. Practicing with different technologies can be a little bit overwhelming, so take some time to research and experiment. Try new creative things, even if they are a little bit scary!

USE YOUR VOICE

Blogging is not always about words on a screen. You can also create a podcast (audio) or a vlog (video). First, let's record some audio! If you have a recorder, try recording yourself saying your name and telling potential listeners about your day. Do this a few times and see what topics pop up. Talking out loud is very different from writing things on paper, and you may feel more comfortable talking than writing. You can even pretend to be a personality on the radio. See what fits with your personal style.

HANDY TIP!

If you have already discovered what it is you want to say and how you want to say it, you are ahead of the blogging game. For others, it may take a while to figure it out. Don't worry—there's no need to rush!

VIDEO YOUR DAY

Once you have recorded some audio, why not try recording yourself in front of a camera? It can be exciting and scary, but it can also be incredibly fun. We will go into more detail in Skill 4, but if you have a phone or a webcam, these are great tools to start playing with. Try recording video of you introducing your pet to your viewers or of you telling a story about what you did last Saturday. Start with anything. Remember, this is just practice and it doesn't matter what you record. Its purpose is to help you become used to standing or sitting in front of a camera.

YOU AND A FRIEND CAN TAKE TURNS FILMING EACH OTHER.

DON'T FORGET YOUR AUDIENCE

Before you get too far into your blog, ask yourself whom you are writing your blog for. First and foremost, you should be writing your blog for yourself. If you are writing for others, you will soon lose interest and get bored. Yet don't forget you will have an audience and they are important too. They will be invaluable as your blog grows. They might suggest ideas to write about or comment on your blog posts. Some might become ambassadors to your site and will recommend it to their friends as well as other people online. Your audience will also help you stay on track. If you have a bad day and you write about it, they will want to help you and keep you writing and blogging. If you have fun with your readers and make them feel welcome, they will want you to succeed.

HANDY TIP!

It's okay to use other blogs as inspiration, but take elements and give them a twist to make them your own!

ALWAYS REMEMBER TO BE YOU!

Let your personality shine on your blog. If you want to write and share your own fiction, blog that! If you think skiing is the best sport in the world, vlog that! No matter what you choose to blog, vlog, or podcast about, do it because you are interested in it and it makes you smile. Once you start showing off how happy you are blogging about the topics you've chosen, your blog will be stronger and will attract followers.

STAY SAFE ONLINE

Most bloggers find the Internet a rewarding and exciting place to be. However, keeping the Internet safe has proven to be difficult. When we communicate with strangers, it is impossible to know exactly who they are, even if they sound fun and friendly. With this in mind, it is very important that you take precautions to protect yourself, especially when you share information through your blog or vlog.

GOOD AND BAD COMMENTS

As much as you want everyone to love your blog, your visitors may not always agree with what you share. They may wish to correct or disagree with you. Many of these conversations can make you feel that you've learned something new, while others may make you feel unwelcome. You can find out more about how to deal with this in Skill 8.

YOUR NAME OR PSEUDONYM

If you intend to share information about yourself with others, consider blogging under a pseudonym or pen name. This means that you never reveal your real name on your blog. Instead, you use a fake name that matches your personality. This works for a lot of bloggers who want to share their knowledge online but don't necessarily want to share their personal life. It can also be great fun giving yourself a new name entirely of your own making!

THINK UP A FUN FAKE NAME THAT SUITS YOUR **PERSONALITY** OR INTERESTS.

YOUR LOCATION

Don't give out your location. If you don't make blog posts about where you live or which city you live in, it can make it hard to guess exactly where you are. If you do want to talk about your hometown, make sure you don't give any information that would pinpoint where your neighborhood or home is.

ADDRESSES AND PHONE NUMBERS

It may seem obvious, but always keep information such as your address and phone number out of your blog posts, podcasts, or vlogs. If you want people to get in touch with you, create a free email account that you keep apart from your personal account.

DON'T FORGET YOUR PARENTS

Your parents can be really helpful if you ever feel unsure or uncomfortable about anything you encounter online. Talk with them about posting photos of yourself or your friends, and always check with them if someone you "meet" online asks to get together in person. Your parents are also the only people you should share your passwords with, and you should always check with them before downloading or installing software. Above all, show them how much fun the Internet can be. Who knows, you might even teach them a thing or two!

IMPORTANT: ALWAYS CHECK WITH YOUR PARENTS BEFORE POSTING INFORMATION ABOUT YOURSELF ON THE INTERNET.

SOCIAL MEDIA SITES

Because you will be using social media channels to promote your blog, you should become familiar with how these sites treat your privacy. Most provide you with tools to maintain a certain level of privacy by restricting who is able to view your posts. You need to be 13 years of age or older to join most blogging and social media sites.

FACEBOOK

Facebook allows users to protect their account and posts by restricting who can see them. You can set your posts to be visible only to your close friends, wider friends, or certain groups you create. To promote your podcast, blog, or vlog, you can always create a new Facebook Page to share those posts. This means that you can promote your Facebook Page publicly while maintaining a level of privacy on your personal account.

TWITTER

If you are using Twitter to talk to your friends or followers, you can make all of your Tweets protected, which means your tweets will be visible to only those who follow you. If someone wants to follow you, they will have to request that you allow them to do so.

HANDY TIP!

If someone sends you a message that you think is mean or makes you feel uncomfortable, don't feel bad; it is not your fault! Tell your parents right away.

GOOGLE PLUS

Google provides accounts for people using some of their products, such as their free email platform Gmail. You don't have to use their social platform either, but if you decide to promote your blog on Google Plus, you can restrict who can see your posts. Just like Facebook, you can promote your blog by using a Google Plus Page. It is easy to set up and can be kept apart from your personal account.

DO SHARE

OTHER SOCIAL MEDIA SITES

There are so many different social media sites out there to choose from, such as Tumblr, Snapchat, Instagram, Periscope, and more. They are great tools to promote your blog, but you should always be aware of what information you share and consider the privacy settings of each. If you find out that your blog's audience uses some platforms and not others, research which tools those platforms have that you can use to protect yourself.

PRIVACY SETTINGS HELP KEEP YOU IN CONTROL!

DO NOT SHARE

KEEPING FAMILY AND FRIENDS IN THE LOOP

Something that is often overlooked is what your friends and even your parents share about you. Sometimes your friends can share your information without your permission, even if you've set restricted sharing on your Facebook or Google accounts. They usually don't do this on purpose, but rather because they want to share your blog with others! It is a good idea to make sure that your close friends and family understand what you are doing online and how they can help protect you as a blogger. Make them aware of the things that you do and don't want shared in public.

WRITE BLOG POSTS

Becoming an amazing blogger depends entirely on how you put together each individual blog post. Sometimes you will want to write a really precise blog post, and other times you will just want to have fun. It sounds simple, but sometimes the creative well can run dry and writing even the most simple of posts can prove challenging. But with the tips in this section and a little practice, writing posts will become a breeze!

WHAT IS YOUR BLOG ABOUT?

When first starting out, you need to choose a topic for your blog. What do you want to talk about? What sorts of things will you share? Your blog can be just for fun, where you talk about silly things or imaginary lands, or it can be a platform for teaching your visitors something, such as how to knit the best scarf ever. All you have to do is make your blog about something you are passionate about. There are an unlimited number of topics you can write about, but it's best to choose one and stay focused.

THE MORE FOCUSED YOUR BLOG IS, THE MORE VISITORS YOU WILL GET!

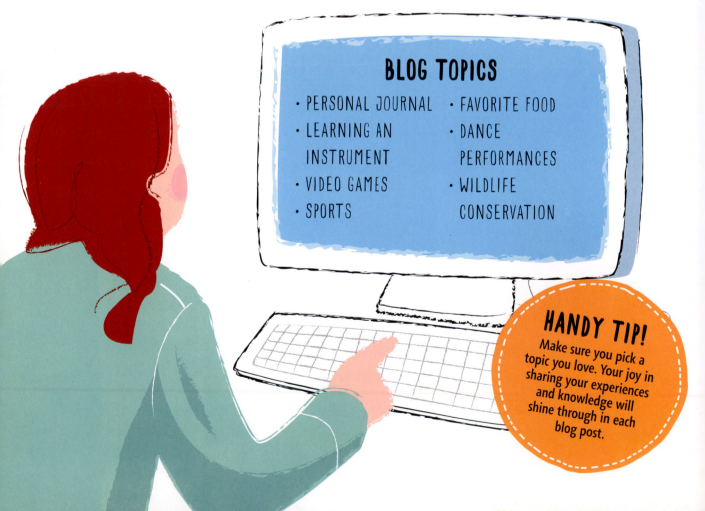

BLOG TOPICS

- PERSONAL JOURNAL
- LEARNING AN INSTRUMENT
- VIDEO GAMES
- SPORTS
- FAVORITE FOOD
- DANCE PERFORMANCES
- WILDLIFE CONSERVATION

HANDY TIP!

Make sure you pick a topic you love. Your joy in sharing your experiences and knowledge will shine through in each blog post.

WAYS TO WRITE ABOUT A SUBJECT

- Tell a story
- Interview your friends
- Share your photos
- Share a dream you had
- Ask a question
- Share your latest adventure

START WITH AN IDEA

With your new blog topic in mind, brainstorm what kinds of things do you want to write about. Let's pretend that you chose doughnuts as your blog's topic. Anything you write on your blog should have something to do with yummy doughnuts. Just like when you are choosing a topic, this list can be endless. The only limitation on how you write about your subject is your ability to remain excited and stay creative. Be adventurous in how you present your ideas and keep your readers coming back for more.

Brainstorm all the things you could blog about that are within your chosen theme.

Here are a few ideas to get your thoughts flowing for your first or next blog post.

THINK OF HOW YOU CAN EXPLAIN YOUR PASSION FOR THAT TOPIC IN MANY DIFFERENT WAYS.

DOUGHNUTS BLOG

Where did the doughnut come from?

How are doughnuts made?

What kinds of soft drinks go with doughnuts?

Are doughnuts baked, boiled, or both?

What's the biggest and weirdest doughnut ever made?

Where is the best place to get a doughnut?

Which kinds of sugar are used in doughnuts?

How many different types of doughnuts are there?

Take a photo of every doughnut eaten.

Go on a doughnut sampling tour and write about the experience.

HANDY TIP!

Carry a small notebook and pencil around with you—ideas for blog posts can pop into your mind at any time! (If you have a phone, you could use that instead of a notebook.)

THE OUTLINE

You should always outline your blog post. Outlining gives you a road map to follow when you start writing and filling in the details. If you jot down your initial thoughts as a list of bullet points on a page, it will help you form more details as you write.

BLOG POST OUTLINE

- **OPENING**
Your first sentence and paragraph. This should help to interest the visitor and keep them reading your blog.

- **PARAGRAPH 2**
A second point about the topic.

- **PARAGRAPH 3**
Your final thoughts about the topic.

- **CLOSING**
A quick summary of your thoughts. You may want to post a question to your visitors in this paragraph or talk about future posts on this subject.

This is a very general and basic outline for a blog post. Your posts will look similar but may have more or fewer paragraphs, depending on how much you want to share. Once you write and upload several posts to your blog, you will start to get into the habit of following your very own basic outline and you will naturally develop your own blogging style.

HANDY TIP!

One of the great things about outlining a blog post is that you may discover you know more than you think. You may also think of future posts! If you do, make sure to jot those ideas down on a separate piece of paper for later.

HOW LONG SHOULD A POST BE?

When beginning your new blog, you should keep your blog posts short—no more than three hundred words. This will get you into the habit of writing concisely. Blog posts need to capture the reader's attention right away and keep them interested until the end.

HOW OFTEN SHOULD YOU POST?

Every blog and every blogger is different. There are blogs that are updated every day and other blogs that are updated once a week. Writing can take time, so you need to be aware of your schedule in order to figure out how often you should post.

THE MORE YOU WRITE, THE FASTER YOU WILL BECOME.

HANDY TIP!
New readers tend to decide within the first few lines whether they are going to continue to read your blog, so make that first sentence entertaining, funny, or unique.

YOUR WRITING PROCESS

When you first start out writing your blog posts, you will hopefully begin to recognize that you have your very own natural writing process. Everybody has their own way of getting ideas from their mind and onto paper or a computer. Each is a unique process, so make sure you start to develop your own. If you write better in the morning, write in the morning. If you write better right after dinner, do that. By writing fairly quickly and posting quite often to your blog, you will start to recognize what helps you write the best that you can.

HOW TO GET THE WRITING DONE

You've got the outline and you're ready to write—here are some tips that will help you get your writing done.

p 1: WRITE SOMEWHERE RIGHT FOR YOU

Some bloggers like to write in very quiet places that allow them to focus and write their blog posts without any distractions. But there are writers who like a little noise in the background—either music or the sounds of a local coffee shop. How you write and what you like to have going on around you as you lose yourself in thought is entirely your own experience. You will have to write several dozen blog posts before you recognize what works best for you.

YOU CAN BLOG ANYWHERE YOU WANT!

Tip 2: WRITE ON A COMPUTER

This is usually where most bloggers start. They begin by typing out their blog posts into a program such as Microsoft Word, then copying them into their blogging software.

Tip 3: WRITE ON A PHONE OR TABLET

This may not be the best way to write full blog posts, but many bloggers have started to jot down ideas—even entire blog posts—on their mobile devices. You can always email yourself the text you write and finish it up on a computet later.

Tip 4: WRITE BY HAND

Many writers and bloggers draft their blog posts by hand. Several bloggers have mentioned that they prefer using pencil and paper to write out their thoughts for a blog post before typing them up on a computer.

Tip 5: FIND TIME TO WRITE

Writing a blog every single day or every other day can take up a lot of time. Setting aside a time to write everyday may not be reasonable because most bloggers have other daily commitments. Instead, you could have a writing day every couple of weeks when you write out several posts at once, and then upload them on different days.

Tip 6: DON'T EDIT WHILE YOU WRITE

When trying to get your thoughts out about your topic, it can be tempting to edit while you type. But try your hardest to push past that feeling. You'll find your ideas come more readily if you just let them flow. You can always return to them afterwards.

HANDY TIP!

If writing blog posts takes up too much time and you are no longer enjoying it, that is a sign to cut back on the number of posts you are writing. If you lose the fun in writing your blog, your readers will notice. Don't be afraid to change your schedule!

EDIT YOUR BLOG POST

Before you upload your posts, let them sit on your computer for a day or two, then take a second look. This time allows your mind to process what you've already written and return to it with a fresh perspective. Taking a break from writing about a single topic is never a bad thing—just don't forget to go back and finish!

Tip 1: PRINT OUT YOUR POST

If you prefer reading on paper rather than the screen, one option for reviewing your blog posts is to print them out and read them that way. It is also good practice to mark up your posts with a pen to get used to finding typos and spelling mistakes.

Tip 2: READ YOUR BLOG OUT LOUD

An impressive blogger trick when editing a post is to read it out loud. This allows you to progress slowly through the text you have written and find places where it could be improved.

Tip 3: DON'T RELY ON SPELL CHECK

When checking your blog post for spelling errors, don't let your computer do all the work. When reviewing your blog posts, you not only need to check for spelling errors, but also for missing punctuation and words.

Tip 4: HAVE SOMEONE ELSE READ THEM

Another option is to have someone else read your blog posts. You can print them out or email them to a person whose judgment you trust. They can give you feedback on how the blog posts flow and whether they cover all the points you want to make.

INCLUDING AN IMAGE IN YOUR POST WILL GRAB A READER'S ATTENTION RIGHT AWAY.

Tip 5: ADD IMAGES

Every good blog post deserves a great image. When including an image in a blog post, it's a good idea to use one central image to represent it. For example, if you write a blog post about your pet rabbit, take a photo of your rabbit and add that to your post. If you write about something you simply don't have a photograph for, you can find blog-friendly images on the web.

USE YOUR OWN PHOTOGRAPHS

The first and best place for photos is your own camera. Take a lot of photographs and use them in your blog posts. Use ones that relate to your post or that represent what you have written. Use your artistic eye to see if your photos will fill your blog post's requirements.

USING OTHER PEOPLE'S IMAGES

If you want to find an image to use that doesn't belong to you, you need to be careful that you have permission to use it. Turn to page 55 to find out more about what you're allowed to use and how to credit other people's content. To avoid being confused as to whether or not you can use a photo, look for public domain photographs. If you can't find a good public domain photograph, try to look for Creative Commons tagged media. This makes using other people's creations easy because all you need to do is follow the rules of the person who created the media in the first place. There are plenty of resources online that you can use to find Creative Commons licensed media.

USE PUBLIC DOMAIN PHOTOGRAPHS

If you are going to use other people's photographs, you need to make sure that you are allowed to use them. The easiest and safest way is to use public domain photographs. Any photographs that are placed in the public domain pool on photo sharing services are free to use any way that you want. You can download photographs, edit them, and use them in any post you write. Here are a few resources you can check out:

- Flickr's Public Domain Pool (www.flickr.com/groups/publicdomain)
- PD Pics (www.pdpics.com)
- Pixabay (www.pixabay.com)

Tip 6: DON'T BE PERFECT!

A written blog post is not supposed to be perfect. Because of their nature, blog posts are written quickly and posted often. They are never static and can be corrected at a later time. Even if you re-read a blog post three months or longer after publishing it, you can always click the edit button and make corrections.

FILM YOUR VLOG

Introducing video into your blog adds a number of exciting opportunities for your creative spirit. Video requires some additional technology: you will need a camera, possibly some lighting, and maybe a microphone to make sure that your voice is strong and clearly heard. If you don't have a heap of equipment, just use a camera or a smartphone and you will do fine!

SCRIPT IT OUT

Unless you are going to talk exclusively about your own life, any vlog you film should have a basic script. This could be as simple as a series of bullet points of things you want to mention during your episode, or it could be very detailed, where much of the information is read to the camera.

YOU DON'T NEED EXPENSIVE EQUIPMENT TO **START A VLOG.**

TEMPLATE FOR A SIMPLE VLOG SCRIPT

- INTRODUCTION
Subjects going to be covered.

- SUBJECT 1
Subject Detail 1
Subject Detail 2

- SUBJECT 2
Subject Detail 1
Subject Detail 2

- CLOSING COMMENTARY

HANDY TIP!
For most vlogs, the simple script is the preferred format, as it won't block your creativity. Letting your personality show is more interesting than reading a list of facts or talking points.

YOUR CAMERA

Now that you've thought a bit about what you are going to say, you are going to need a camera to say it to! Many beginner vloggers will ask the question "what camera should I use?" The simple answer is that you can use any camera. Video cameras can be expensive pieces of equipment and require a lot of care. For a majority of vloggers, a simple webcam will work great. It will allow you to record directly to your computer, where you will be editing your vlogs as well.

CAMERA OPTIONS

WEBCAMS

Webcams are fairly inexpensive cameras that you plug into your computers. If you are lucky enough to have a laptop, it will probably come with a webcam built in. The quality of the cameras may vary, but for a simple vlog they will do the trick.

TABLETS AND MOBILE PHONES

You can also shoot video on most smartphones and tablet computers. Filming on these types of devices may be a little more challenging because you will need to keep them as steady as possible. They are suitable for beginner vloggers.

COMPACT CAMERAS

Small point-and-shoot cameras with the capability to film video are also decent cameras with which to experiment. Like smartphones, these types of cameras are easy to carry around and can be used to shoot a vlog when the mood strikes.

VIDEO CAMERAS

Video cameras are great for personal vlogs as they provide the most features and capabilities for video, but they are also the most expensive. If you don't have one, you could ask if your school has one you are allowed to borrow. If you have access to one, that's great, but you'll get on just fine without one.

HANDY TIP!

You might want to start by filming a vlog in which you sit in front of the camera while talking and showing selected props. Once you get the hang of vlogging, you could plan some creative action and move around with your camera.

SETTING UP YOUR VLOG SET

The biggest hurdle you will face when starting your vlog is visual composition. This is a fancy way of saying what your vlog looks like. Ideally you want your set to look interesting. Having a blank wall or filming in the dark could look pretty dull, so take a bit of time setting up your vlog's set so that it looks its best. Here are some simple things you can consider before you start shooting.

FOREGROUND

This is where you are. You are in front of the camera and presenting your vlog episode's material. Most often, you will be in the foreground of your vlog's shot.

MIDDLEGROUND

This is the space right behind you. Many vloggers will have something behind them to set the scene and make the shot interesting. This could be a lamp, a chair, a sofa, or maybe a table. You shouldn't have too much in the middleground, or it may distract your viewers. Sometimes it will be nothing at all because you may be shooting your vlog with a close-up.

BACKGROUND

This is what people will see behind you while you vlog. It will take up the full frame of your vlog. If you are inside, this will usually be your bedroom wall, a bookshelf, or some artwork hanging on the wall. If you are shooting outside, it will be the rest of the space you are filming in.

TRY OUT THE **RULE OF THIRDS!**

⅓ ⅓ ⅓

⅓ ⅓ ⅓

THE RULE OF THIRDS

Something else to consider when setting up your camera is the rule of thirds. What this means is that when you are looking through the camera lens you should divide your camera's frame into thirds using imaginary lines. When you film yourself talking to the camera, you will want to position yourself slightly to one side rather than in the center of the frame. Using the rule of thirds makes your vlog appear more balanced and interesting. Most often, vloggers will pay close attention to where their face is, but that doesn't mean you should always stay in a single position.

USING PROPS

Using props can enhance your vlog and add some variety to your post. You can stage a conversation with a cuddly toy, bang a drum while speaking, or even change your outfit every minute throughout your vlog episode. But when using a prop, make sure it makes sense for the topic you are discussing.

MOVING OR SITTING STILL?

The majority of vloggers have their cameras sitting still while shooting their vlog so that they can control the quality of the image and sound. But there are some bloggers who move around as well. Dancing or changing your position while talking to the camera can add excitement, as does walking around while filming (vloggers usually call this "vlogging and talking"). Though this can bring its own set of challenges with lighting and audio quality, finding a quiet place to vlog while being outside in public is a great idea. It creates an interesting atmosphere and backdrop. Just make sure that you are always aware of your audience—keep yourself in full frame and make sure that you can be heard.

HANDY TIP!
Experiment in more than one location. You may find that some locations are too loud and drown out your voice, while others may be too dark for you to be seen.

MAKE SURE YOUR MOVEMENTS DON'T INTERFERE WITH YOUR ABILITY TO SPEAK.

LIGHTING

For your viewers to be able to see you properly, lighting is also important for making you and your background visible. Lighting for vlogs is not always necessary and can be difficult to set up if you are filming outside. Using natural light is actually preferred by a lot of vloggers—it provides a more natural look in your vlog. If you don't have time to shoot in the daylight, using artificial light may be your only choice.

THREE-POINT LIGHTING

Most of your vlog episodes will only require a single light source. As long as the viewers can see your face and understand the information you are sharing, you don't need to get fancy with your lights. But understanding how professional vloggers use lights is useful and will provide you with knowledge you might need in your vlogging future. Filmmakers and vloggers alike use what is called the three-point lighting system.

HANDY TIP!
When you're starting out, it's best to keep things simple. Experiment with the lighting in your own home, filming in different locations to see what natural lighting works best without having to set up any additional lighting.

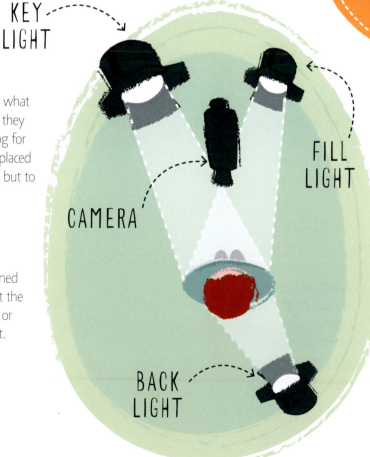

KEY LIGHT

KEY LIGHT

This light is usually what most people use if they are just doing a vlog for fun. This is a light placed behind the camera but to one side.

BACK LIGHT

This light is positioned behind you to light the back of your body or the background set.

CAMERA

FILL LIGHT

BACK LIGHT

FILL LIGHT

A fill light is also placed behind the camera, but on the opposite side of the key light. The fill light helps to remove any shadows on your face caused by the key light.

OUTSIDE VERSUS INSIDE

But what if you want to shoot your vlog outside? Setting up and controling lighting outside can be difficult. The good news is we have the Sun. The Sun is the best light source available to vloggers—it is just a question of where the Sun is when you are filming. The quickest trick for the best lighting is to make sure the Sun is behind the camera most of the time. It may not always be possible, but it is a good rule of thumb.

The Sun is your best light source.

SOUNDING AWESOME

When recording a vlog, a lot of vloggers change their voice on purpose to heighten their personality. Making yourself "bigger" than you are in real life can be more interesting to watch and can hold the attention of the viewer for longer. The trick is not to overdo your performance. One way to think about it is to pretend like you are on a stage.

If you watch someone on stage and compare it to someone on your favorite television program, you will see that stage actors do big actions and even bigger voices in order to allow the audience to see and understand what they are saying and doing. It will take some practice to find your vlogger voice, but don't be afraid to try a few different voices before settling on the one that you and your audience like best.

SINGING!

Who doesn't like a great voice or song? Using music can be a powerful option for making a great vlog post. You can write your own songs, make a cover of another artist's song, or talk about what music means to you! Showing off your talents will always bring visitors back for your next episode.

SILENCE CAN BE POWERFUL

Noise is great, but silence in a vlog can be very powerful when used correctly. Beware of using this dramatic technique too often, though; when you go silent in a vlog, people may think your sound has cut out and go to another person's vlog instead.

MOST IMPORTANTLY, BE INTERESTING!

Regardless of what equipment you have, how many lights you need, or what kind of video quality you have, the key to your vlog's success is to be interesting. This can seem like a tall order, but if you follow the few simple rules for being in front of a camera that were covered in this chapter, you will be able to create a performance that people will love watching.

VIDEO EDITING SOFTWARE

The most challenging part of creating a vlog is the editing process. It can take you a long time and many vlog posts to master the skill, but don't let this stop you from trying. Most editing software will have similar features, but here are the most important ones.

PREVIEW PANES

This is where you will be able to see the video you have shot. Some editing software will have more than one preview window.

MEDIA LIBRARY

Also sometimes called the 'clips library', this is where all of your footage for your vlog will appear. You can include images, your video clips, and even audio clips.

TIMELINE

This is where you will spend most of your time. Editing video will require you to move clips along the timeline, cut sections of the video, and remove parts you don't want. You may also edit the quality of the video, add transitions between clips, and perform some special effects work.

EDITING TIPS

Editing a vlog will take time to master—there are many techniques to learn and experiment with. Two video editors you can use are iMovie (on a Mac) or Windows Movie Maker (on a PC). There are a few simple tips that you can use to make your vlog posts interesting:

JUMP CUTS

Jump-cutting is a quick cut from one moment in your video footage to another. Most vloggers use this technique to remove footage they think is not valuable and to shorten their vlogs to keep them a certain length.

SPEED UP YOUR VIDEO

Speeding things up can be an interesting way to skip through some of your footage rather than throwing it away.

SLOW YOUR VIDEO DOWN

Slowing your video down can have funny results and may give you a moment to bring attention to one of your points.

ADD TEXT

Text can be useful if you are doing an instructional vlog, emphasizing a point, or having a laugh. Just make sure the text is on the screen long enough to be read.

ADDING OVERLAY PHOTOS OR VIDEO

A neat trick you can do is to overlay video while you are still speaking in the background. It will add another layer to your commentary.

EXPERIMENT WITH DIFFERENT METHODS OF EDITING TO SEE WHICH ONES HELP YOU GET YOUR POINT ACROSS.

HANDY TIP! If you want to try something in your vlogs, try it! If it works, you've discovered a new technique to apply to future vlogs. If it doesn't work, you don't need to do it ever again. You will have the satisfaction of trying and learning something new.

RECORD YOUR PODCAST

With blog posts in your pocket and vlogs scripted and filmed, you can now venture into becoming a podcast personality! Podcasts are a bit different from the other types of blogs because they rely entirely on audio. There is nothing for the audience to read or see. This leads to some very different creative options for the podcaster. Let's warm up our vocal cords and get recording!

WHAT WILL YOUR PODCAST BE ABOUT?

What subjects are you going to talk about on your podcast? Will it be a similar theme to your written blog? If so, you are ready to go! But if you want it to be different, choosing a theme can make your show easier to create and more engaging. You can record a show about anything: discuss the types of insects in your backyard, interview members of your family, or simply talk about your day. You could also create a series of shows about a single topic, where each episode describes a different aspect of that topic.

HANDY TIP!

If someone sends you a suggestion, make a list of potential show topics. Remember to write down any new ideas you have in a notebook or on your mobile phone.

HOW MANY HOSTS?

Podcasts come in all shapes and sizes—some feature a single presenter or host, some feature two or three co-hosts, and some feature more than ten co-hosts all talking about the same thing! Having more than a few hosts can be a little confusing, so it's more manageable to create a podcast with only one host to begin with. You can always add more later!

INVITE A GUEST

Maybe you have decided that you don't want a co-host all the time. In that case, perhaps an occasional guest is the answer for keeping your podcast fresh and fun. Try inviting a close friend to your podcast and see what happens. You can learn a lot, gain insight into their thoughts, and listen to their fascinating stories. You can invite other vloggers, bloggers, and even your family to be guests on your show. Pick a topic, send an invitation to a guest, and let the fun begin!

MOST COMMON FORMATS

There are many different elements that you need to decide upon before committing to a show format. Let's see if one of these typical podcast formats works for you.

SINGLE HOST / PERSONAL COMMENTARY

This format is like having your own radio show. You get to pick the topics, make a few notes, and talk them out. You can walk around outside or sit in your bedroom while you record your audio. The key is that this show is all about you.

SINGLE HOST / INTERVIEW WITH GUESTS

This format is similar to the above, but you also include someone who you think is interesting. You can ask them questions and get their opinion about the topic you've chosen.

SINGLE HOST / EDUCATIONAL INSTRUCTION

With this format, you instruct listeners in how to do something. Being able to learn something from your podcast is a great way to attract followers.

CO-HOSTS / INTERVIEW WITH GUESTS

Similar to the single-host format, but with two or more hosts! Each host can interact with the guest and ask them questions about the topic being discussed.

CO-HOSTS / DISCUSSION COMMENTARY

Chatting with another human being is a good way to stimulate conversations between people and provide different perspectives.

TO CO-HOST OR NOT?

Should you have a second host for your show? It is worth giving this some thought because there are a few clear benefits to having a co-host:

- Listeners may find the conversation between you and your co-host to be more interesting than just you speaking alone.

- Multiple hosts can help with all the work it takes to record and post a podcast on a semi-regular basis.

- You can bounce ideas for episodes off each other.

- It can be fun to make a podcast with a friend if you have shared interests.

ONCE YOU HAVE CHOSEN THE FORMAT OF YOUR PODCAST, YOU CAN LOOK AT HOW A PODCAST IS ORGANIZED.

ANATOMY OF A PODCAST

Podcasts come in all kinds of formats, but each has a usual order of what happens throughout a show. Here are a couple of different styles to help you figure out what your show will sound like.

COMMENTARY SHOW

1. Opening comments
2. Musical introduction (on ramp)
3. Welcome message and announcements
4. Commentary and conclusions
5. Closing music (outro / off ramp)

HANDY TIP!
Make a list of interesting people you know among your friends or family. Often a guest with something to talk about can provide the topic for a show.

INTERVIEW SHOW

1. Opening comments
2. Musical introduction (on ramp)
3. Welcome message and announcements
4. Segment 1 (this could be commentary, interview, or scripted performance)
5. Segment 2 (this could be commentary, interview, or scripted performance)
6. Segment 3 (this could be commentary, interview, or scripted performance)
7. Conclusions
8. Closing music (outro / off ramp)

HANDY TIP!
If you want to keep your show topical, you may want to talk about news events or things that are going on around your school or neighborhood.

HOW LONG IS YOUR SHOW?

When hosting a podcast, you should decide how long the show will be. Some podcasts are a few hours in length, but shows often do better and gain larger audiences when they are shorter. Some popular podcasts are as short as fifteen minutes. When planning out your podcast episode's content, don't forget to leave room for your introduction theme and your closing theme.

SOMETIMES **LESS IS MORE:** DON'T WORRY IF YOUR PODCAST IS SHORT.

TAKE TIME TO PLAN WHAT YOU'RE GOING TO TALK ABOUT IN YOUR SHOW. REMEMBER: **CONTENT IS KING!**

YOWL...

SPEAKING OF THEME MUSIC

Like broadcast radio programs, podcasts usually feature a theme tune. If you can play an instrument, you could write your own and record it for your podcast. If you can't, maybe have a friend who is musically inclined and would love to write your theme tune help out. You can even help record it. Just remember, theme music should be fairly short and simple, and you must not use music that belongs to someone else (see page 21).

HOW OFTEN?

One of the things that makes a podcast successful is how often its episodes are released. Like any blog, releasing more often always attracts listeners. However, it may take a bit longer to create a podcast than it would to write a blog entry, so releasing them often may become problematic. Choosing a fixed release day can be the solution to any podcast woes, as it will give your listeners a weekly (or monthly) present.

CHOOSING YOUR RECORDING EQUIPMENT

Now that you've figured out your format, it's time to start recording! You may not know it, but recording audio isn't as difficult (or expensive!) as you may think.

USING MOBILE DEVICES

All you really need is a microphone to get started. Luckily, mobile phones and tablets have microphones built in! Most mobile phones have their own recording software, but you can always install some if you have a smartphone.

LOCATION

Where are you going to record your podcast? Just as when filming a vlog, you need to have a suitable location where you can record without too much background noise. People want to hear your marvelous voice—not the sound of traffic!

"REAL" MICROPHONES

If you want to get a better microphone than the one in your mobile device, there should be a wide variety at your local electronics or musical instrument stores. You can purchase anything from a simple computer microphone all the way up to a broadcast-quality microphone (the microphones you see at radio stations). It is up to you to decide on what kind of microphone you get, but just remember that microphones can be expensive and you should only invest when you know podcasting is what you really want to spend your time on.

STEREO SOUND VERSUS MONO SOUND

When you start playing with audio recording, you will see references to mono and stereo. Stereo uses two or more audio channels to create the impression of sound heard from various directions, as in natural hearing, whereas mono has audio in a single channel. If you are recording audio in stereo, you will be able to adjust the recording to mono in your audio editing software.

ALL YOU NEED IS A MICROPHONE TO **GET STARTED!**

STOP THE ECHO

The major recording issue you may experience is the echo that's produced by the room you are in. The ideal room to record in is a room with fabric-covered furniture, such as a living room. Recording in a room with many flat, hard surfaces is not the best choice. Recording in rooms like the bathroom or a garage can give your voice a lot of background echo and reduce the quality of your audio, which could possibly drive your audience away.

CLOSETS MAKE GREAT RECORDING BOOTHS

Surprisingly, one of the best places to record in is your closet. If you can fit into yours, the clothes inside will muffle the sound and reduce the amount of echo, giving you a clear and high-quality recording.

STOP THE "POP"

Something you may notice when recording audio for either a video or a podcast is that saying the letter "P" or the letter "B" can sometimes record an annoying popping sound. To stop this from happening, you can either buy or build your own pop filter or use your finger!

A pop filter is a circle or square that is covered in a light fabric. The filter lets the sound of your voice through, but stops the air from your mouth from making the popping noises. It softens the sound but doesn't change it enough to stop people from understanding what has been said.

The second (and cheapest) way to stop the popping noise is to place your index finger in front of your lips and hold it there while you are speaking. This is a simple way to divert the air out to the sides. It may take a bit of time to get used to using your finger and learning where exactly to hold it, but the effect is the same as with a pop filter.

EDITING YOUR PODCAST

Editing a podcast is the process where you can clean up the sound quality, remove extra parts that you don't need, or add some additional pieces such as introductions and musical cues. All you need is an audio-editing software package. There are a great number of audio editors available. Many of them cost quite a bit of money, but there is a very popular editor that comes highly recommended called "Audacity." You can download Audacity for free (audacityteam.org), and it contains all of the tools you need for audio editing.

HANDY TIP!
If you want to generate MP3 files, you will also need to install the LAME editing library. This will allow you to import and create your own MP3 files.

DEFAULT AUDIO FORMATS

With some mobile devices, you will notice that the manufacturer has set the default format the audio recordings will be saved as. These formats are chosen to save space, but they are not podcast-friendly. When you are recording on a mobile device, test out the audio recording to see which kind of file it creates. See "file formats" on the next page for help with this.

EDITING BASICS

Editing audio is similar to how you edit video. Most audio editing software will have three basic parts to it:

THE EDITING TOOLBAR

The editing toolbar contains all of the tools you will need: the play and stop buttons, audio levels indicator, and custom audio filters.

THE TIMELINE

This is where all of your audio tracks are displayed. From here you can drag audio tracks forward and backward along the timeline in order to mix them together.

THE PROJECT RATES

The final section contains the audio settings, time counter, and information about the quality of your audio tracks.

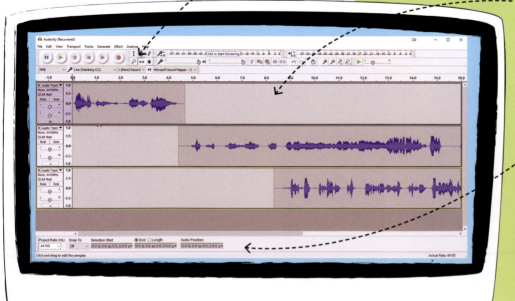

FILE FORMATS

Just like video, audio has different types of files you can use to share your podcast. You may encounter one of these file formats with your recording software:

- **MP3** This is the most common audio file format. It is the recommended format to share your podcast.

- **M4A** Most iPhones and iPads record in this format.

- **3GP** Many Android and non-smartphones record in this format.

CONVERTING TO MP3

Your audio editing software can usually convert file formats for your podcast. If you recorded your audio in a different format, open the audio file you created in your audio editor and then save it as an MP3. For now, MP3 files are the most common format downloaded by podcast listeners. In the future, more formats may be made available, but saving your file as an MP3 will allow you to reach a larger audience.

PLAY WITH SOUND

Something that a lot of podcasters don't do is play around and experiment with sound. Try recording your podcast in a very echo-y place to create a unique sound. Release a podcast where you conduct an interview in a coffee shop or a shopping mall that has a lot of background noise to make listeners feel like they are there too. You can even try playing with other sound effects. Get brave and try out something new every episode. You can then explore the different editing techniques needed to get the best out of your audio.

SQUARK

SQUARK

SQUARK

SQUARK

POST YOUR BLOG

You've done it! You have chosen your topic and written a few blog posts. You may have also recorded and edited a couple of episodes for your podcast or vlog. Now you need to pick a site for your blog to live.

WHERE TO POST YOUR BLOG

Deciding the best place for your blog can be difficult. Choices include software packages that you can install, expensive platforms that you can use, and many free blogging systems that get the job done just fine. For this skill, we're going to focus only on the free ones. Each free blogging platform has it strengths, so it's a good idea to explore each of them before making your final decision.

BLOGGER.COM

This is Google's blogging platform. It is one of the oldest platforms and is one of the most robust and flexible. You can share all kinds of content and connect it to your YouTube and Google accounts for easy sharing of your photos, videos, and text.

WORDPRESS.COM

This is an incredibly popular blogging platform that gives a lot of bang for your blogging experience. The Wordpress system provides a free account; however, unlike Tumblr and Blogger, it will cost money as your blog grows.

TUMBLR.COM

Tumblr is owned by Yahoo! and is a very popular place for blogs of all kinds. You can share text, photos, audio, and video all in a single platform. It is a good place to start experimenting with your content.

HANDY TIP!

Don't over-think your posts! You can always go back and make updates, such as improving your introductions and changing your photographs.

YOU CAN BUILD YOUR VERY OWN BLOGGING COMMUNITY, SO GET **STARTED TODAY!**

YAY...

BUILDING AND POSTING YOUR FIRST BLOG POST

Every journey begins with the first step. For your blogging career, the first step is to write and post your first blog entry. Once you have written your post, there are a few rules that are important to follow for any post you're planning to publish.

1. USE A CATCHY TITLE

Having a funny or catchy title can help attract people to read the entire post. Have fun with your titles. Don't settle for the bland and boring—give them action and excitement! Using humor is also a great way to persuade people to click.

2. ADD PHOTOGRAPHS

Why not take a photograph of something related to what you are writing about? Try to make the photograph as eye-catching as you can. If you have a great title and a great photo, people are more likely to visit your blog.

3. INCLUDE AN EXCERPT

There is a secret to blog posts that is sometimes missed: most great blogs have a really great introductory paragraph. Readers have short attention spans, so you should hook them with your first words—make them funny or thought-provoking. In addition, the introductory paragraph is often used to advertise the blog on search engines and on your website.

4. POSITION A VIDEO

Including a video in your blog post can be done a few ways. The quickest is to use the embedding code from the video sharing service. Placing the video part way down your blog post will give you space to introduce the topic of the blog post and what the video is about.

UPLOADING VLOGS

When your very first vlog entry is ready, you will need to upload it to a video sharing service such as YouTube or Vimeo. These platforms make your videos accessible to the widest audience possible.

MAKING YOUR VIDEOS ACCESSIBLE

Making your videos unique and easy-to-find will make people more likely to watch them. Here are some key ways to do that.

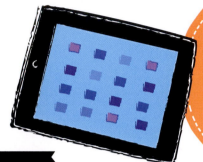

HANDY TIP!
Keep your videos organized and shareable. It won't be long before you are experimenting with new ways to share your thoughts and ideas with potential new readers.

Tip 1: THUMBNAILS

After you have uploaded to YouTube, you will notice that a screen capture of the video is used to show people what the vlog may be about. Unfortunately, these captures can be boring and not attractive to your blog audience. Creating a visually interesting thumbnail for your videos can help your vlogs stand out.

INSERTING VIDEO

Once you've uploaded your video to YouTube, you can include it on your blog. All you need to do is to copy the embedding code from YouTube and paste it into your blog. Most blog platforms will have a quick way for you to add the code, so take a look at the instructions to see what your blogging platform prefers.

Tip 2: PLAYLISTS

Organizing your vlog posts into helpful playlists can help your audience find your videos. You can sort them by topic, date, or almost any other way you can imagine.

Tip 3: EMBEDDING

After you have posted your video, you will have a few sharing tools to use. The main sharing tool (and the tool you will need to use to put your video into your blog post) is the embedding tool. This tool creates code that you can use to add your vlog into the blog post.

WHAT FILE SIZE?

The embedding code may have some customization options for sizes and quality. You can select what you feel is best and add into the blog post. Videos with a high resolution (and a bigger file size) will be higher quality, but will also take up more space on your computer and take longer to upload—particularly if you don't have a very fast Internet connection. Keeping your videos to 30 minutes or shorter and at a medium resolution will help speed things up when editing and uploading the files.

PLACEMENT

Where should you place the video? Some people think the best place is at the top of the blog post and others think after a written introduction works better. Take a look at blogs with similar topics to yours and see how they are laid out. There is no one answer for placement. Remember, as long as the video is present and visible, your visitors will find it.

- - - - - - - - - - - - - - - - -

SHORTCUTS

Some of the blogging platforms provide you easy ways to insert videos uploaded to YouTube. You may be able to use just the main video link and not have to worry about the embedding code (but it is a good idea to be familiar with the embedding code as well).

LIVE STREAMING

A newer option available to video bloggers is the live stream. With live streaming, you can record a vlog while chatting live with people who watch your videos. Live streaming gives you new and interesting ways to interact with your audience. Here are the main live streaming sites:

YOUTUBE (www.youtube.com/live)
This is the largest platform for sharing videos. It provides you with the ability to not only store and share videos, but also to host live events.

TWITCH.TV (www.twitch.tv)
Twitch is a video streaming service targeted at gamers. If you like to share gameplay videos and want to interact with your audience while you are playing a game, this platform can be amazing for you.

PERISCOPE (www.periscope.tv)
Periscope is a platform created by Twitter that allows you to stream video live to the Internet. You can perform your show and stream it to your audience but after 24 hours the video is deleted.

MIXLR (www.mixlr.com)
Mixlr is a live streaming site that lets you stream audio to the world! All you need to do is click record and your stream is live on their site. You can embed the live stream into your blog, and you can even share your recorded shows on your own website (if you have one).

ADDING AUDIO

Adding audio podcasts to your blog is very similar to embedding video. The main difference is that you want to make it possible for the visitor to download the audio file because most software used for listening to podcasts needs to be able to find and use the audio file you post.

One of the quickest ways to get your podcast online is to use the Internet Archive (archive.org/index.php). This is a free system that allows podcasters and video bloggers to host and share their audio and video. It is particularly good at hosting audio files because once you upload your audio, it converts the file into a variety of different formats.

GETTING AN EMBEDDING CODE

Once you've uploaded your file to the Internet Archive, you will be able to use their embedding tool (much like YouTube) to embed your audio file with an audio player that your visitors can use.

PLACEMENT OF YOUR AUDIO PLAYER

You will need your player to be visible to your audience. However, its placement isn't as important as the video's since many people use podcast listening software to enjoy audio programs instead of viewing them on a computer screen.

INCLUDING A SHORTCUT

A link that leads directly to your audio file should also be present. This allows podcatchers to find and download episodes of your podcast quickly.

USING THE INTERNET ARCHIVE

The Internet Archive is a great place to host both audio and video if you don't want to use YouTube. It allows you to store, listen, view, and share your digital media for free, forever. It also gives you a free location that you can then embed or link to on your blog.

TAGS

Tagging your content with appropriate keywords is a great idea. This adds keywords to your blog posts and allows your audience to search your site based upon the keywords you've assigned. For example, if you write twenty posts about your pet dog and you add a tag of "dog" to those posts, anytime someone visiting your site clicks on the tag, all of the tagged posts will be sorted and presented to your reader automatically. You can use tags to organize your blog and combine different types of content together. You can bring podcasts, vlogs, and text blogs together under one single tag. It can be very handy!

SHARING YOUR POSTS

We will talk about this in more detail in the next skill, but it is good to remember that once you have completed your blog post, you will want to share it with the world. This means you will want to post a link to your blog post on Facebook, Google, and Twitter. This will give people a quick way to find your posts and will allow them to share the posts quickly too!

CHASE

FRIENDSHIP

ANIMALS

CUTE PUPPY

PET TRAINING

DON'T FORGET TO TAG YOUR POSTS!

FIND YOUR AUDIENCE

Writing and recording a solid blog post is only the beginning. If you've got something to say, then chances are you'll want someone to hear you. Your audience is going to be anyone who reads, watches, and listens to your blogs, vlogs, and podcasts. With all of the different social platforms available to anyone using the Internet, gaining attention can be a tricky thing. There are some things you can do to raise your profile and get yourself noticed.

WHO IS YOUR AUDIENCE?

Identifying your audience is really important. Who are you hoping to talk to? How old are they? What sort of things are they into? Are they male or female? What interests do they have? What do you have in common with them? Where do they go online? Asking yourself these sorts of questions—and any others you can think of—and writing down as much information as you can about your typical audience member can be a really useful way to talk about things that will appeal to them. This is a technique used by lots of companies and organizations to talk in a way that will interest their audience about things that are relevant to them.

HANDY TIP!

When you've created a profile of your typical audience member, give them a name, grab a random photo of a person from a magazine or online to represent them, and pin it to your wall for future reference.

TALK TO OTHER BLOGGERS

One of the quickest ways to gain an audience is to connect with other bloggers who write, vlog, or podcast about topics you enjoy. You can interact with them by commenting on their blogs or their social media. Bloggers love talking about their topics and most will want to discuss them in more detail with other interested bloggers. Take a chance and let experienced bloggers know that you're starting your own site and you would love to hear their thoughts. However, don't be a spammer and ask their visitors to come to your own blog. You need to add something to their conversation too.

HANDY TIP!

If you choose to talk to the right communities on the web, then it's easy to start talking with people you don't know. If you're into the same things, then they'll most likely be interested in what you have to say!

KEEPING YOUR AUDIENCE

Here are some more tips on how to interact with your audience in a positive way and keep them coming back for more.

Tip 1: ALWAYS REPLY

If someone has taken the time to ask you a question, you should always take the time to respond, if possible. There are many different ways to communicate online, so you should make it clear how you would prefer people to contact you. If you prefer people to send you an email, or if you like to chat via Twitter, make sure you say that on your blog. Also try to check your comments every day to see if anyone has started a conversation. It can be hard work keeping up with an audience, but it can also be very rewarding.

Tip 2: CHAMPION OTHERS

As blog communities grow, there will always be stand-out personalities who keep conversations lively and entertaining. A good way to build your reputation as being open and friendly is to recognize and praise the most active community members on your blog.

Tip 3: KEEP OLDER CONTENT

Include links to older content somewhere on your site or make sure you refer to them in newer blog posts. New visitors to your site might be interested in seeing older posts, and you'll be able to see how your blogging has changed over time.

DON'T STOP LEARNING!

It is never a bad idea to learn new things. Since you have a blog and are writing, recording, and talking about your ideas every day, you should try to learn more about your chosen topics. Reading other blogs that talk about the same things as you do will help you add more knowledge to your blogging arsenal. You will be able to pick up new bits of information and add different perspectives to your website.

It is also important to share your new knowledge. Let people know that you read a new book or followed a great blogger! Keep your ears and mind open to new information and then turn that information into blogging gold.

HANDY TIP!

Every once in a while, look over your old blog posts and note ways of improving what you wrote. This review and critique of your own work can help you improve the way you write future posts.

ASK QUESTIONS

Don't feel like you have to know everything. Some people will say that if you ask a question on the Internet, especially when you are writing a popular blog or vlog, you may lose readers because they expect you to know everything about your blog's topic. But the truth is that people often like to share their knowledge with you. Ask questions directed at particular bloggers or members of your readership. Try to be as specific as you can, and don't forget to ask follow-up questions to start a dialogue with others. You may be surprised at what you get in return!

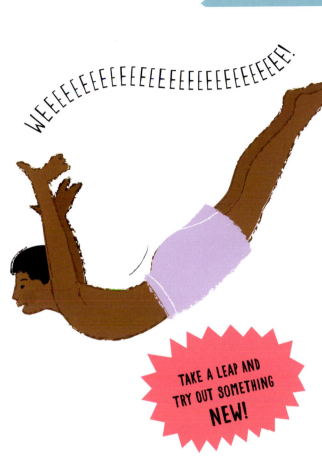

WEEEEEEEEEEEEEEEEEEEEEEEEEEEE!

TAKE A LEAP AND TRY OUT SOMETHING **NEW!**

TAKE CHANCES

Be brave with your blogs; sometimes the craziest ideas can turn out to be the most interesting blogs of all. Don't forget that anything original or unique will stand out. Sometimes you may want to talk about a tough or uncomfortable topic for you or your audience. Don't automatically discard the idea; review what you have to say and find a positive spin on it. Even the hardest of topics can be tackled and recorded with a smile. Be an advocate for awesome and write those tough blog posts—there is always a silver lining to the hardest writing. All you need to do is take a breath and find it. Don't forget, you can always turn to your audience for help. It may be that the topic is just as difficult for them!

STAY POSITIVE AND SEEK ADVICE

Any seasoned blogger will tell you to stay positive even if you find it difficult to discover new topics. When interacting with others online, don't forget to keep a positive attitude. You may be facing a frustrating experience or just be having a bad day, but don't let your audience know that—unless you want some advice! There is nothing wrong with letting your followers know how you are feeling and asking for advice about what to do!

KEEP YOURSELF INTERESTED

Don't forget that your most important audience member is you. Lots of writers fall into the trap of writing only for their audience, but if you find yourself getting bored by your own writing or discover that the topic you've chosen simply doesn't interest you, trust your instincts and move on. It can get very hard to maintain your blog if you stop writing for yourself—then it stops being fun!

GETTING SOCIAL

How you plan to be social online is just as important as writing regular blog posts and filming your vlogs. Getting involved and building a community around your blog can go a long way toward gaining attention for your site.

TELL YOUR FAMILY, FRIENDS, AND NEIGHBORS

Believe it or not, the best way to guarantee that people will view and read your blog is to share it first with people you see almost every day. Let them know when you start and when you post, and ask them to spread the word. You will be surprised how much traffic you can get early on simply because you laid the groundwork through word-of-mouth.

EMAIL

One easy way of getting the word out about your blog is to include information about it at the end of all of your emails. Most email programs have a way of recording a default signature that gets automatically added to each new email.

TWITTER

Twitter is a great place to have conversations with others in real time. It works much like texting on a cell phone, but many of the conversations you have are open for others to read and add to. Using Twitter is a quick way to interact with your followers and notify people that you've posted a new blog post. Having open conversations with the world provides a route for new readers to find you.

IMPORTANT!
YOU MUST BE AT LEAST
13 YEARS OLD
TO SIGN UP FOR FACEBOOK, TWITTER,
INSTAGRAM, TUMBLR, AND FLICKR
(WITH YOUR PARENT'S PERMISSION).

FACEBOOK

If you already use Facebook, you understand how your comments and postings can get the attention of your friends. It is like having a virtual word-of-mouth system available to you all day and every day. If you are old enough, then setting up a Facebook Page for your blog can be an awesome way to provide a space where people who like your blogs and vlogs can get together to discuss what you've written or recorded. Facebook also has a number of communities or pages that may be related to your topics. Make sure you join up and start some new conversations!

INSTAGRAM

Instagram is a popular photo-sharing service connected to a large community of people who love to talk to each other about visual styles. It's a mobile-only platform where you can take photos on your mobile device, apply unique visual filters to your photos, and share them on Twitter, Facebook, and other social sites. You can have conversations, shoot short videos, and let people know what you are talking about on your blog!

FLICKR

If you are looking for a more robust place to store your photos, Flickr is the most popular photo management platform available to bloggers. You can store, share, host, and organize your photos. You can even create and embed photo albums to get the attention of new people.

HANDY TIP!
Flickr loves photographers! If you are out and about taking a lot of photos on your camera, why not share them?

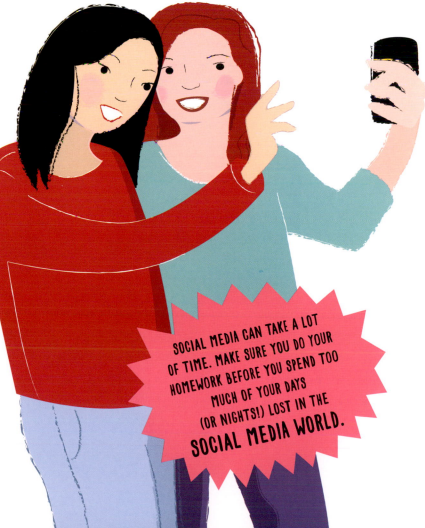

HANDY TIP!
With so many different free platforms to choose from, it can be hard to decide which ones are best. Take a chance on any of them and see what works best for you.

SOCIAL MEDIA CAN TAKE A LOT OF TIME. MAKE SURE YOU DO YOUR HOMEWORK BEFORE YOU SPEND TOO MUCH OF YOUR DAYS (OR NIGHTS!) LOST IN THE SOCIAL MEDIA WORLD.

TACKLING PROBLEMS

If you blog for long enough, you will eventually run into a few hiccups along the way. Technology will break, the Internet will not work properly, and some members of your blogging audience may not act as you hoped. To keep blogging stresses to a minimum, you can do some of these things to avoid any issues before they start.

INTERACT WITH YOUR AUDIENCE

When blogging first started, there were only two ways to talk to your blogging audience. You could talk to them through email or chatter with them through the commenting system connected to your blog. Today we have all kinds of services like Twitter and Facebook where people will want to chat and talk with you. Even though these services are on other websites, you can always apply your own rules.

SET GROUND RULES FOR COMMENTS

Your blog is your space on the Internet, so you make the rules. Many bloggers set out a post on their blog that has a list of rules their members must follow.

Your rules can be basic or very detailed, and how many rules you have is up to you. You can set out a few rules to begin with and change them whenever you feel it's necessary. You can also apply these rules to communities you establish on social media websites.

MY WEBSITE RULES
- Be kind.
- Do not use bad or negative language.
- Don't make fun of other members.
- I will delete comments that do not follow the rules.
  - Most importantly, be respectful of others.

HANDY TIP!
Think of yourself as a king or queen. It is your job to make a list of rules that visitors to your website are required to follow.

MANAGE COMMENTS

Comments are important to all bloggers. They help you to understand what your audience members are thinking. You can interact with readers in a very personal way by having conversations via the comment system on your blog. Unfortunately, comments are vulnerable to spam and can be a place where arguments arise. You will need to monitor your comments to remove spam, delete negative posts, and, most importantly, respond to comments!

GLITCHES

Broken equipment, garbled recordings, and a failed Internet connection will plague even the most prepared blogger. You may be recording a video or editing a podcast episode and—boom—out of nowhere you lose everything! The trick is to stay positive. You may lose your edits or maybe even an entire blog post, but that is okay! You can always rewrite what you typed into your laptop or pick up the recorder again and try to remember all of the brilliant things you said the first time. If you are a vlogger and you simply forget to press the record button, all you can do is take a breath, press record, and record that perfect vlog episode all over again. It happens to every blogger—you will not be the first to suffer from a failure of technology!

DEALING WITH TROLLS

A troll is usually someone who posts unnecessary, negative comments on your blog and social media channels. They can be annoying partly because of the negative things they say, and partly because they want to direct any and all discussions toward them. More than anything, trolls love being the center of attention.

How do you deal with a troll? Remember when we said that you are king or queen of your blog? The first rule is to simply delete any comments they leave on your blog. You don't need to have permission to get rid of anything. If a troll leaves a negative comment about anything to any of your other readers, just delete the comment and try to ignore them in the future.

Some commenting systems allow you to prevent people from leaving comments based on their email address or account info. You can add them to an ignore list or add keywords to your comment filtering system that prevent comments with certain keywords from being posted. You will need to look into the commenting system of the blogging platform you are using to see how to do this.

DEALING WITH CYBERBULLIES

Trolls can be annoying because all they really want is a little attention from whoever responds to their taunts. Bullies, on the other hand, can be more intrusive and usually have a target. Unfortunately, being a blogger makes you a fairly large target. If someone feels that what you are writing or recording is worth their time, they can make your online life uncomfortable. Bullying in any form is something that you should never put up with but, unfortunately, if you don't know who is attempting to bully you, it can be hard to stop them.

The best rule you can follow for dealing with cyberbullies is not to engage with them. Do not respond to their comments, regardless of how negative and untrue they are. Talk to an adult about the situation. Do not think about what they have posted and, above all, push on with your blogging. It is important to recognize that you can't make everyone happy. Stay positive and remember that your real audience will build you up—a few negative people can't destroy that. As bloggers who want to share and provide information to people about the topics we love, we need to be strong!

HANDLING COMPLAINTS

Sometimes you will have to be a referee and help out members of your community. Unfortunately, not everyone gets along all of the time. Since you want to have a happy and relaxed online community, you will need to make sure that you are prepared to help out when conflicts arise. Treat all members of your community with respect and listen to each complaint because you can learn something about your community and potentially create new rules to help.

START CONVERSATIONS

Sometimes people may say something within the comments of your blog that makes you sad, mad, or happy! They may even ask questions that you think deserve answers. Don't be afraid to write a blog post about something someone said in the comments of your site, in a tweet, or on Facebook. Make it known that you are listening to your visitors by using some of their thoughts to create new thoughts of your own!

MAKING CORRECTIONS

Bloggers who write and record long enough will make mistakes. You may say someone's name wrong in a vlog episode, or you may mistake one thing for another in a daily post. The great thing about blogging is that you can make corrections! You can edit your older posts and correct the mistakes, or you can record newer vlogs and mention that you made an error.

SPEAK TO A TRUSTED ADULT ABOUT ANY COMMENTS ON YOUR BLOG THAT MAKE YOU FEEL **UNCOMFORTABLE** OR UPSET.

BLOGGING ETIQUETTE

As your blog becomes more popular and you watch your audience grow, there are a few things that you should do to maintain good relations with readers and other bloggers. Being active in online communities, being aware of what you can and cannot do with other people's content, and respecting people in your community all show that your blog is a positive place for people to visit.

COPYRIGHT AND OTHER PEOPLE'S CONTENT

When you are writing a blog post or jotting notes down about your next vlog episode, it might be tempting to copy or use footage from other bloggers' vlogs or blog posts. You may be inspired by other bloggers and think it is a good idea to use part of their content to enhance your own. While that can be okay, there are rules to follow. These are outlined on the opposite page.

HANDY TIP!
When taking your own photographs, you don't always have to set up and prepare for the perfect shooting conditions. Life is messy, so don't be afraid to capture it with your lens. Be spontaneous!

DON'T USE PHOTOS STRAIGHT FROM A SEARCH ENGINE OR FROM ANOTHER PERSON'S SITE WITHOUT PERMISSION.

USING SNIPPETS OF TEXT

If you want to use another blogger's words to enhance your own blog post, it is always a good policy to use only short snippets of text and link to where the text came from, in case your readers would like to know more about the blogger who wrote it. Use the same rule when using content from news agencies as well.

USING PHOTOGRAPHS

Many beginner bloggers want to use photographs to make their blog posts look great. Yet, one of the first mistakes beginners make is to use photographs they don't own. To avoid this, you should always do one of two things: ask permission to use another photographer's imagery or take your own photographs! (see page 57) You will always have time to capture the perfect image for your blog posts if you take your camera everywhere you go. Take pictures of buildings, flowers, people, puppies, and scenery. Taking photographs every day will help populate your personal photographic catalog. Even if the photo doesn't match your blog post perfectly, you can usually find something that works. Who knows, maybe another blogger will ask to borrow your photograph for their next blog post. You can make a lot of connections with other bloggers when you share the wealth of your own photographic library.

USING VIDEO CLIPS

If you want to include some video from another vlog, you must ask permission from the creator. Make the clips you use short and to the point. Don't copy long clips of video from other vloggers, and make sure you let your audience know where you got the video clips from.

LINKING TO SOURCE MATERIAL

If you use content from another blogger, you must link to where you got the material from. Linking to the source also lets your audience know which bloggers you enjoy and like to visit.

CREATIVE COMMONS

When bloggers began to be noticed by wider and wider audiences, the Creative Commons was formed. This allows bloggers and other content creators to post a license on their site to notify any visitors or other bloggers what they can or cannot do with the content (see page 57.)

ASKING PERMISSION

Many bloggers who are starting out think that just because a photo, video, or blog post is available to them online, it gives them permission to use that content on their own website. If you are not sure if you can use content from another blogger or another source on the Internet, ask for permission. If you do, provide as many details as you can about how you would like to include their content on your blog. Some bloggers will let you use their content, while others may have their own rules about how their content can be replicated. But if they say no, you should respect their wishes.

REMOVAL OF CONTENT

If you have used content from another blogger and they don't want you to, the best policy is to remove the content, re-edit or rewrite what you have made, and repost it. Most bloggers enjoy the attention, but some will want their content to appear only on their own blog.

BEING A GOOD NEIGHBOR

Everyone wants to live beside a great neighbor! The same can be said for bloggers. Every blogger wants the same thing: a strong, helpful audience. Yet, you won't be able to build a great audience if you are not a great blogging neighbor. Here are a few suggestions to help you become a great blogger neighbor.

Tip 1: ADD TO CONVERSATIONS, DON'T SPAM

When leaving comments on other bloggers' blogs, don't simply ask their community to visit your website. Many online communities prefer that visitors add to the conversations being had. If you are not participating in the conversation, it may be better to leave no comment at all. Adding to a chat or conversation in the comment system of another blog or jumping into conversations on Twitter, Google Plus, or Facebook can help you become part of a community.

Tip 2: SHARE LINKS

One of the things you can do to encourage a strong blogging community is to share links to other bloggers' sites. Some bloggers will only do this if they have a post they want to promote, but sharing blog posts that you like simply because you think they are great can make you popular! If another blogger on the Internet mentions that your blog has value and should be visited by their audiences, getting to know their blog in return and sharing it with your community is an amazing way of promoting strong bonds between blogger communities.

Tip 3: CREATE A BLOG LIST

Similar to sharing links to blogs you like, building a list of blogs you love to read is also a neighborly thing you can do. There are billions of blogs out there, and sharing a list of those that you find interesting can help your blog community grow.

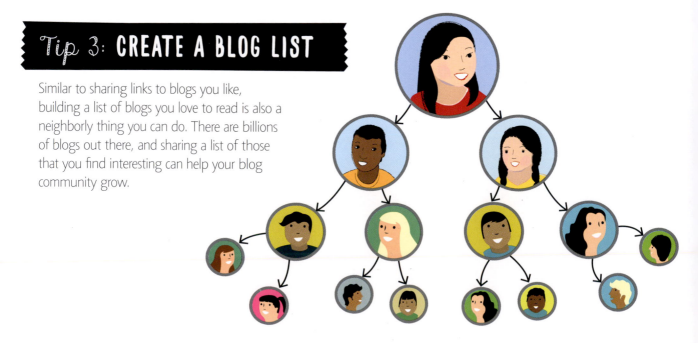

Tip 4: INSPIRE AND BE INSPIRED

Not every idea you have will be a spark from out of the blue. Most ideas you have will be inspired by someone else. Ideas can grow from reading a good book or a great poem, or even watching other bloggers. If this happens to you, making reference to where the idea came from and sharing a link to that source will add to your level of awesome. You may feel self-conscious about where your inspirations come from, but you shouldn't. Building a community and sharing in other people's success always reflects well on you.

Tip 5: SAY THANK YOU

When people share links to your blog or leave nice comments thanking you for your latest vlog, take the time to say a simple thank you. Saying thanks to someone you don't know can go a long way toward making them smile, and hopefully they will continue to say nice things about your blog in the future.

FREE RESOURCES

Remember the importance of using only photographs and other media that you own? Well, the good news is that if you don't have the perfect image for your blog posts, or if you need something to inspire you, there are resources on the Internet that you can use free of charge. Many are covered under the Creative Commons (mentioned on page 55).

THERE ARE PLENTY OF OTHER SOURCES—IT IS JUST A QUESTION OF WHAT YOU NEED TO MAKE YOUR BLOG POSTS **AMAZING.**

PIXABAY (WWW.PIXABAY.COM)

Pixabay is a large collection of public domain photos that you can freely use for your blog.

FLICKR'S CREATIVE COMMONS POOL (WWW.FLICKR.COM/CREATIVECOMMONS)

Photographs in this collection are covered under the Creative Commons. This means many of the photos you can use for your blog posts, but you will need to credit the original authors and add a link to their work.

FLICKR'S PUBLIC DOMAIN POOL (WWW.FLICKR.COM/GROUPS/PUBLICDOMAIN)

Like the Creative Commons pool, this collection contains thousands of photos you can use for your blog. The only difference is that these photos have been put into the public domain. You can use any of them without crediting the source.

SOUND BIBLE (WWW.SOUNDBIBLE.ORG)

A royalty-free resource for those who would like to add sound effects to their vlogs or audio podcasts.

KEEP BLOGGING!

Now that you are well on your way to becoming an expert blogger and vlogger, let's go over some skills you need to keep your blog moving forward. It can take time to build a successful blog, so you will need to be both patient and persistent. Blogging can sometimes feel like hard work, but you can avoid feeling overwhelmed and stressed in lots of different ways. Remember: blogging should be fun and rewarding!

MAKE YOURSELF SMILE

It's important to stay connected to the things that you find interesting. When you're thinking about ideas for your blog, make sure you check to see if the ideas you write down make you smile.

Try this out!

FINDING A GOOD BLOG IDEA

1. Think of an idea.

2. Look at yourself in a mirror.

3. If the awesome person staring back is smiling, work on that idea!

4. If they look bored, maybe write down your idea and store it away for the future.

5. Review your saved ideas once a month.

YOU DON'T HAVE TO KEEP YOUR BLOG THE SAME AS WHEN YOU STARTED. YOU CHANGE OVER TIME AND SO SHOULD YOUR BLOG.

Doing this simple exercise will prevent you from getting bored with your writing. You may surprise yourself—the idea you write down may not cause you to jump for joy today, but perhaps it will next week, next month, or even next year.

SCHEDULING

Writing every day can be difficult. You may not have enough time in your day to do all the writing you want to, so making a writing schedule can help, especially when you need to film vlogs as well! Here are some alternatives to keep your writing going.

MAKING TIME FOR YOUR BLOG

- Schedule a day every two weeks when you write several posts in one sitting.
- Schedule an hour a day where you do nothing but write your blogs.
- Schedule a reading day or, better yet, schedule an hour a day for nothing but reading.
- Schedule a day for the filming and editing of your vlogs. (You need more quiet time for recording any audio or video!)

HANDY TIP!

If you've got other things going on in your life, give yourself a break and start up again when you have more free time.

BE READY FOR INSPIRATION!

Do you remember any moments when you were out shopping or visiting friends at their house and an idea popped into your head? For bloggers, remembering these insights of brilliance is important, and you will want to be prepared. Always carry a small notebook and a pen or pencil, your camera for video or photographs and, if you record audio, your audio recorder as well. Having these items will not only help you record your thoughts but also keep your brain working and ready to record and create at a moment's notice!

SOME FINAL TIPS

Keep your blog fresh—for you and your audience—by living your life to the fullest. The more connected you are to the world, the more interesting your blog will be.

Tip 1: WRITE IN DIFFERENT PLACES

Writing outdoors, at a friend's house, at school, or simply in a different room in your own home can do wonders for keeping your thoughts fresh and positive. Changing your location and surroundings can help clear your mind and give you back your focus!

Tip 2: TAKE A WALK

Exercise is an amazing tool to help you get your words organized and ready so you can put them down on paper or onto a digital camera. Taking quick walks can help you stay strong for long days spent filming your vlog or writing many different blog posts at once.

Tip 3: READ MORE

Developing a reading habit will help you generate blogging ideas faster and more often, so set aside time every day to read a book (fiction or nonfiction—it doesn't matter) and take your mind to a different world.

Tip 4: BE OPEN

New experiences are all around you. The trick is not to think too much—just do them. If you notice a new social network, sign up. If you have a local baseball team, go see them play. If a local art gallery is having an event next weekend, head on down. Seize the day!

Tip 5: TAKE A RANDOM CLASS

There is always something new to learn. Baking, learning about history, creating art, or even learning an instrument can expand your mind and help you think "outside of the box." And you never know who you are going to run into when you're there!

Tip 6: EXPERIMENT AND DON'T BE AFRAID TO MESS UP!

There are times when you will stand in front of your bathroom mirror asking yourself: "Oh no! What was I thinking?" But bloggers who don't take risks become boring. Be more afraid of asking yourself: "Why didn't I do that?"

Tip 7: PAUSE

Taking time to sit quietly can be a powerful tool. Sit and read, listen to music, or look out your bedroom window. Sometimes you just need to refill the mental fuel tank.

Tip 8: JOURNAL

Try writing down things that you wouldn't want to post on the Internet in a private journal instead. This will keep you in touch with yourself and clear out unwanted or unproductive thoughts.

Tip 9: MOST IMPORTANTLY—BE YOU!

Putting your thoughts and feelings out into the online universe can be scary. But revealing to other people that you are a human being on this planet, complete with your own set of thoughts and feelings, is rewarding and will teach you loads about yourself and your world. So whatever you blog about, good luck, be brave, enjoy, and most of all, be you!

BE WHO YOU WANT TO BE, NOT SOMEONE YOU IMAGINE OTHERS WANT TO SEE!

USEFUL LINKS

WHERE TO POST YOUR BLOG

blogger.com
Google's blogging platform is one of the oldest out there, and is also one of the most robust and flexible.

wordpress.com
The most popular blogging platform on the web.

tumblr.com
Owned by Yahoo!, this is a very popular place for blogs of all kinds, and is excellent for experimenting with content.

LIVE STREAMING

youtube.com/live
The largest online platform for sharing videos.

twitch.tv
A video streaming service aimed at gamers.

periscope.tv
A platform created by Twitter that allows you to stream live video onto the Internet.

mixlr.com
A live streaming site that lets you stream live audio to the world.

HELPFUL TIPS FROM YOUTUBE VIDEO CREATORS

youtube.com/yt/creators
Learn how to build production skills, understand your audience, improve your channel, and connect with other creators.

AUDIO EDITING SOFTWARE

audacityteam.org
This is a free, easy-to-use, multi-track audio editor and recorder.

ADDING AUDIO

archive.org/index.php
Internet Archive is a free system that allows podcasters and vloggers to host and share their audio and video.

GOING SOCIAL

twitter.com
A great place to have conversations with others in real time.

facebook.com
Using this social media site is like having a virtual word-of-mouth system available to you all day and every day.

instagram.com
A popular photo-sharing service connected to a large community of people who love to talk to each other about visual styles.

flickr.com
The most popular photo management platform.

PUBLIC DOMAIN PHOTOGRAPHS AND SOUNDS

pixabay.com
A large collection of public domain photos.

flickr.com/creativecommons
You can use any of the photographs in this collection, as long as you credit the original authors.

flickr.com/groups/publicdomain
You can use any of the photographs in this collection without crediting the source.

soundbible.org
A royalty-free resource for those who would like to add sound effects to their vlogs or audio podcasts.

GLOSSARY

AUDIENCE/FOLLOWERS group of people who read, listen to, or view works you create and post on your blog

BLOG series of text, images, videos, or audio where individuals or groups of individuals write and share their thoughts, opinions, and experiences. Entries are arranged in reverse chronological order.

BLOGGER COMMUNITY / COMMUNITIES audiences who support a blogger or group of bloggers

COMMENTS messages created and saved on a blog visible to other individuals on the Internet

COPYRIGHT exclusive right given to the creator of a work to publish, sell, or share a work

CREATIVE COMMONS recognized copyright system that allows creators to dictate how others use their content

EDIT action of making changes to a post by removing or adding content

EMBED inserting a video or audio player using HTML-based code that you copy from a social media service like YouTube, Twitter, or Facebook and paste into a blog editor

GLITCHES sudden and unexplained software error

LIVE STREAM live transmission of video or audio over the Internet

MIND MAP a diagram created to organize and connect ideas

MP3 type of audio file. The most common format currently available.

MP4 type of audio or video file.

PLATFORM web forum that enables people to post blogs or vlogs

PODCAST series of audio episodes

POSTING action of uploading, usually by typing information into a blog post

PROPS objects used in the filming of a vlog or other video

PSEUDONYM / PEN NAME a pretend or fake name or identity

PUBLIC DOMAIN media that is free to use because its copyright is expired or forfeited

RENDER process of saving a video file once editing is complete

SHOW FORMAT structure of a vlog or podcast

SOCIAL MEDIA websites and applications that people can use to share text, audio, and video in their social networks

STAGE where the edited or potential final product of editing is visually represented

TAG / HASHTAG / KEYWORD words used to organize data or posts on a blog

TIMELINE location within video and audio editing software that visualizes the flow between clips

UPLOAD transmission of a media file from a computer to an online location

VIDEO CLIPS short clips of filmed content that are used to build a final video edit

VLOG series of video episodes

INDEX

My big idea